Absalom

by

W.B. Godbey

First Fruits Press
Wilmore,
Kentucky
c2018

Absalom.
By W.B. Godbey.
First Fruits Press, © 2018

ISBN: 9781621718192 (print), 9781621718000 (digital), 9781621718208
(kindle)

Digital version at https://place.asburyseminary.edu/godbey/17/

For all other uses, contact:

First Fruits Press
B.L. Fisher Library
Asbury Theological Seminary
204 N. Lexington Ave.
Wilmore, KY 40390
http://place.asburyseminary.edu/firstfruits

Godbey, W. B. (William Baxter), 1833-1920.
  Absalom / by W.B. Godbey. – Wilmore, KY : First Fruits Press, ©2018.

    pages 33 ; cm 21.

    Reprint. Previously published: Greensboro, N.C. : Apostolic Messenger
    Office, [190-?]
    ISBN: 9781621718192 (print)

    1. Absalom, Son of David.   I. Title.

BS580.A35 G62 2018   221.92

Cover design by Jon Ramsay

asburyseminary.edu
800.2ASBURY
204 North Lexington Avenue
Wilmore, Kentucky 40390

First Fruits
THE ACADEMIC OPEN PRESS OF ASBURY SEMINARY

First Fruits Press
The Academic Open Press of Asbury Theological Seminary
204 N. Lexington Ave., Wilmore, KY 40390
859-858-2236
first.fruits@asburyseminary.edu
asbury.to/firstfruits

ABSALOM

By

W. B. Godbey

AUTHOR OF
"New Testament Commentaries." "New Testament
Translation," and a great number of
other books and booklets.

PUBLISHED BY

THE APOSTOLIC MESSENGER OFFICE

GREENSBORO, N. C.

ABSALOM

During the seige of Rabbah, the capital of Ammon,
by the Hebrew army under Joab, David was caught
by Satan, who managed to get his black lasso over
his neck, superinducing his precipitation from the
heights of holiness, where he had walked with God
since his juvenile shepherdhood, meanwhile his faith
was so heroic as to enable him to slay the monstrous
lion, and the huge bear and wind up his nomadic ser-
vice in the decapitation of Goliath, the champion of
the Philistine army, who had stampeded the host of
Israel forty days by his constant challenge, with the
acquiesence of his nation to settle the conflict in a
hand to hand battle with the champion of their
choice. When Jesse sent out David with some love
tokens to his three brothers in Saul's army and to
hold a class meeting with them and see whether any
of them had lost his hold on God, when this huge
monster, clothed in shining steel, an invulnerable
panoply from top to toe; his spear, like a weaver's
beam, sword, battle-ax, all glittering in the effulgent
beams of that brilliant Syrian sun, when, lifting up
his stentorian voice he shouted like the roaring lion,
"Why prolong this effusion of blood gratuitously and
the enormous expense of these two great armies?
Why not send me a man to cross swords with me and
bring this bloody war to an end in a hand to hand
combat? If he whips me, we will all be your ser
vants; and, if I conquer him you will serve us. Si-
lence, profound as the grave, interrupted by sighs
and groans every where prevails. The shepherd boy
can stand it no longer, but speaks, "Why does not
someone accept this challenge and take away the
dark opprobium from the Hebrew banner? Why
shall this uncircumcised Philistine thus browbeat the

armies of the living God? We must have a fight, to take away the reproach from Israel. If nobody else accepts the challenge, count me in at once; though but a stripling, I cannot see Jehovah's banner thus trail in the dust while the daughter of the uncircumcised doth triumph."

(a) Now his brothers castigate him, "You little fool, go back to those few sheep, we know your vanity, coming out here to see the battle;" meanwhile others run like racehorses to the king and tell him, "There's a fellow out here who says he will fight the giant," when he shouts for joy, as they were all so intolerably chafed by his impudence, which they had endured forty days, that they would do anything to have a fight with him, rather than longer bear the odium of cowardice, which he was throwing in their faces, each revolving day.

Consequently he says, "Bring him to me at once." On arrival he says, "And do you propose to fight that giant?" "Oh," says he, "of course, I will if you can do no better, anything to remove the reproach of Israel." "Why," says Saul, "thou are but a stripling, and he a mature man of war, so infinitely thy physical superior." "Oh," says David, "the God of Israel who delivered into my hands the roaring lion and the huge bear, when they came to devour my flock, so I slew them on the spot, will also deliver this giant." As he was utterly unarmed, having nothing but a sling with which he threw rocks, to protect his flock, and it was in his pocket out of sight, Saul proceeds at once to invest him with his panoply, the best armor in the nation; but it was entirely too big for him, so he could not use it, and consequently took it off and walked away to meet the giant, thus utterly unarmed, and when he accepted his challenge, he thought it was a burlesque turned on him for his ridicule, and consequently execrated him in the name

of the Philistine gods, observing, "I'll settle you at
once and feed you to the dogs," which he would have
done if David had come in reach of his panoply; fire-
arms having never yet been dreamed of. As we read
about "700 men in Benjamin all lefthanded and so expert in hurling stones with their slings, that they
could throw them to a hair's breadth and not miss,"
so David was thoroughly drilled in the sling exercise.
Crossing the brook intervening he picks up a few
smooth stones and puts one of them in his sling,, and
whirls it rapidly around his head in a whizzing circle
to give it momentum, adroitly lets it fly, aiming at his
eyebrow just below the impenetrable steel helmet
protecting his head, at that place where the brain is
so nigh, and consequently is darted right up into his
brain, killing him instantly; David moving like a
streak of lightning, taking his sword, cutting off his
head, puttng it on his spear and carrying it back to
the Hebrew army, all making the mountains on eith-
er side the Elah valley roar and reverberate with
their shouts of victory; meanwhile the Philistine army, ignoring their obligation to surrender, all stam-
pede from the field, runnng like they were shot out
of cannons, every man for his home, and the men of
Israel after them, chasing them all the way to Gath,
the giant's home, Ekron, Askalon, Gazah, and Ash-
dod, slaying them as they fled; and afterward turning and spoliating their camps.

(c) At this time Saul was not acquainted with David and he asked Abner, his chief captain, who he
was, and he could not tell him. Consequently he had
to introduce himself, "I am the son of your servant
Jesse the Bethlehemite." This wonderful achieve-
ment took him forever from the sheepfold, to the
leadership of the nation, making him the shepherd
of Israel. God had wonderfully blessed and saved His
life the seven years, meanwhile Saul was after him to

kill him; because even the songs of the women as they greeted them on their triumphant return from the victorious battle of Elah, leaping and singing their congratulatory national airs, "Saul has slain his thousands and David his myraids," aroused the jealousy of the king, so he concluded that in that boy he had a competitor for the crown, which he wanted to transmit to his son Jonathan, and to remain in his family through the oncoming ages, till the sounding of the last trumpet; even giving him his daughter Michal in wedlock, in order to have him slain by the Philistines, as he contracted with him for a hundred Philistine scalps as a dowery, from the fact that he was poor and could not give anything but his labor, at the same time feeling sure that the Philistines would kill him while he was killing a hundred of them.

(d) Accepting the contract, he darted away and in a single campaign brings back two hundred scalps and demands the king's daughter, who of course is given. Though he then chased him seven years, like a partridge over the mountains, till he finally left his country and went away to Philistia, when he ceased to pursue him, and as the years roll on, finally was crowned king of Israel at Hebron; Saul, having, after a reign of forty years, fallen on Mt. Gilboa, and leaving the crown to his son Ishbosheth, who, after five years, was assassinated by Beneus and Hypher, who carried his head to David at Hebron, thinking that they would receive a princely fortune; but as David was a man after God's own heart, who was always true to God, as the Word says, "Except in the case of Uriah;" therefore instead of the anticipated reward, he simply obeyed God's commandment in reference to all murderers, having them executed, thus taking out of the country the innocent blood they had shed when they murdered the king; thus pleasng his subjects so surprisingly, as they saw that he was the man they needed to protect them and rule over them, sent for him to come from Hebron where he had reigned seven and one half years over his own tribe, when they crowned him king of all Israel.

(e) Thus reigning with wonderful efficiency, victory everywhere perching on Israel's banner, to the surprise of himself and all the world, Satan got the run on him in the case of Uriah, lassoing him completely and crushing him beneath his cloven foot, blackening him from top to toe with the awful iniquities of adultery and murder; having like a weasel, stolen a march on him in the vain delusion, that he could thus utilize his royal prerogative, oblivious of the immutable fact that sin is the same in the king as in the beggar, and God is no respector of persons. He remains a backslider a whole year, when God in His mercy verified the trite maxim, that He is married to the backslider, in signal mercy favoring him with the ministry of Nathan, the prophet, who went into his house and looking him in the face, as every preacher must do, or lose his soul, and in a very simple parable, gave him the truth in a nutshell.

(f) "In a city there lived a very rich man, whose herds and flocks and every other species of wealth superabounded. In the same city lived a poor man who owned but one sheep, a beautiful ewe lamb, which he treated like a baby and consequently the pet lamb actually appeared super-human in his humble hovel. A sojourner stops with the rich man and he wants to feed him; so instead of going to his own flock, he takes the innocent, lovely, beautiful, fat lamb from the hut of his poor neighbor and slays it to feed his visitor." Having related the story to David, thinking that it occurred in his own kingdom, he decided that the rich man should be slain and fourfold remuneration given to the poor man. When Nathan looks him in the face and says, "Thou art the man." The brilliant intellect of David took in the whole affair, at once. The light poured into his soul and he saw his awful ruin, as Satan had caught him in a trap, and ruined him. Then Nathan, as he had heard from God, told him that He would show him mercy and that He would take from him the bright little boy, then but a few months old, the idol of his heart. Consequently the child took sick and though David prayed, wept and mourned, pleading for his healing as long as he lived, when he was dead, he responded, "I shall go to him, though he shall not return to me." 2 Sam. 12. Read Psalm 51, and you see his radicl repentance, going down to the bottom, confessing the turpitude of his fallen nature, the swift and prolific precursor of all his appalling catastrophes, which rushed on him with crushing and irresistble avalanches of guilt and condemnation., v. 5. "I was shapen in iniquity and in sin did my mother conceive me," as the Methodists have been singing two hundred years,

"Lord, I am vile, conceived in sin,
Born unholy, and unclean;
Sprung from the man, whose guilty fall
Corrupts his race and ruins all."

Here his frank and unapologetical confession, "Against Thee and Thee only have I sinned, and done this evil in thy sight; cleanse me with hyssop and I shall be clean, wash me, and I shall be whiter than snow. Then will I teach transgressors thy ways, and sinners shall be converted unto Thee."

(g) While his repentance was radical and thorough and his restoration beautiful, triumphant and glorious; yet as his example was so detrimental and unapologizable, God said to him thru Nathan the pro-

phet, "The sword shall never depart from thy house."
It was not long till the awful trouble in the case of
Ammon, his son, and Tamar, his daughter, half
brother and sister, took place, which reflected so un-
apologetically on the former and the same time not
only the profligacy, but the subsequent maltreatment of the latter was really a heart breaking calamity, and we all commend her full brother, Absalom,
for his kindness, giving her a home in his own house;
but must condemn the awful retribution inflicted on
Ammon, whom he treated so courteously as to remove all supicion of the terrific retribution, which he
inflicted on him, after waiting two years, when he
manipulated a sheep shearing frolic, and by permis-
sion of his father, got all of his brothers to attend it,
and there in the presence of the whole family, except
David, whom he tried to have with them;and when
Ammon was merry with wine, responsively to an ar-
ranged plot, hired assasins slay him in the midst
of their festivity; the news reaching the palace, that
all the king's sons were slain, and nearly killing David till it was corrected by the information that none
but Ammon was killed.

(h) Of course Absalom fled into exile, going to his
mother's people in Syria, where he stayed three years
when Joab suborned a widow of Takoah to wait on
David with a parable which he had put in her mouth,
giving a fictitious parallel case, so identical, that it
told its own story before she got through, as it ap-
plied to Absalom's case and had the effect to move
the parental heart of David, lest he might die there
in exile; whereas it was actually impossible to bring
back the dead brother and so many people actually
felt that he was justifiable in killing him, which was
untrue, as he actually usurped the prerogative of the
civil officer. Therefore the result of Joab's instru-
mentality, utilizing this poor widow, weeping over

the two sons, the one dead and gone and the other in
lonely exile, David gave his consent for him to come
back to Jerusalem, to his home, yet never inviting
him to the royal mansion nor even looking on his
face, till three years rolled away, then five years
since he had seen him or he had been in the royal
palace. Thus Absalom those three years, though at
home was in the attitude of a criminal, and really in
more infelicitous environments than when in exile;
Joab dodging him to avoid the responsibility of recon-
ciling his father to him; so he long tried to meet him,
in order to prevail on him to serve him in that so
much desired reconcilement, that finally he fired Joab's field, when he at once came to see him, to know
what it meant, when he confessed that it was a simple dirty resort to get to look in his face, as everything else had failed, and he was so anxious for the
reconciliation of his father to take from him the criminal stigma. Then Joab acquiesced and proceeded
at once to the work of reconcilement, which heartily
reciprocated, telling him that it was all right and to
bring him along to his house; whom on arrival he received kindly and lovingly, impressing on his cheek a
copious fatherly kiss, after an alienation of five
years.

Chapter One.
HIS BEAUTY.

The Bible tells us that Absalom was actually the
most beautiful man in the nation; physically perfect,
without a solitary blemish any way at all, really the
bean ideal of mascular symmetry, and so recognized
by everybody; his raven black hair, so copious and
beautiful, that he cultivated it with cosmetical in-
genuity, transcending even the coquettery of the
fairer sex, i. e., the princel coxcomb of the age; his

hair, which he clipped once a year, actually weighing
three pounds, (it seems incredible, but we have the
plain statement. I trow, that when he had it clipped
he carefuly preserved it, and, as the Orientals so
much appreciate facial ornamentation, attached se-
veral year's clippings together and used them on spe-
cial occasions in the way of ornamentation.)

(i) While his hair was the most copious I have
ever heard of in all my life and among Orientals
highly appreciated in the way of ornamentation, and
hence proved in his case a wonderful incentive to his
pride, it also played a conspicuous part in is death;
and his mule ran under a very tangled, brushy, tenacious oak tree and precipitated his head up among
those contorted and matted branches, catching him
and holding him fast meanwhile the animal ran away
and left him hanging, doubtless, suspended by that
copious suit of hair.

After his reconcilment to his father and restoration to unimpeachable sonship, he proceeds at once
to rise early in the morning, as the Jews in all lands
have always been the most stirring people and are
today; rising long before day and coming to Jerusalem in the bright early morning to catch the top of
the market. Therefore following this mutual pa-
ternal and filial reconciliation after an alienation of
five long years, it seems he made a new departure,
taking on fresh courage and even then the incipient
aspiration to the kingdom, begins to crop out, as he
adopted the habit of rising very early, taking his
place in the gate of the city, the moment the keeper
unlocked it and catching all the people as they came;
speaking to them lovingly, kissing every man and
kindly saluting all the women, thus introducing himself favorably to all the people in Palestine as they
came to the capital and metropolis, so frequently.
As they knew he was the king's son, and his own

person so majestic, actually as the Bible says the
finest looking man in the nation, they all not only
appreciate his acquaintance but thought of things
they wanted in the way of royal favor and told him.
In every case they found him patient, bright, intelli-
gent, and shrewd in the diagnosis and solution of
all financial and religious problems; responding to
them courteously and complacently, "Your matters
are good but there is no one in the kingdom appoint-
ed to adjudicate them; if I were king, I would be delighted to attend to everything the people want in
the way of securing their rights, privileges and
prosperity; thus Absalom stole the hearts of the
people." His beauty, affability, sociability, and es-
pecially the deep interest he seemed to take in everybody, won their hearts, till he not only became acquainted with almost everybody but actually mag-
netized them, till they fell in love with him; actually
enamored, with his loving palaver; so that all hearts
became centralized on him as the ultimate successor
of his father on the throne; meanwhile the murder
of his brother Ammon instead of provoking their
condemnation, actually weilded a potent influence
in favor of his royal promotion as the popular sympathy was unanimously with Tamor whom Ammon,
treated so unapologizably, diabolically, not only in
her ruin but the unpardonable austerity and actually demoniacal cruelty which followed; thus upon the
whole giving Absalom a favorable introduction to the
whole nation, commendatory of his anticipated king-
ship, as they saw that he had the grit to enforce law
and order regardless of the ties of consanguinity
even in the highest circles of nobility and royalty.

(j) All young people should take warning from
Absalom's sad and awful fate which seemed really
to originate from pride, inspired by his personal
beauty, which proved a snare ultimating in his ruin

for time and eternity. 1 Peter 2 ch, we find the encouraging statement that the wife really has the power to save her husband even though he be an infidel; of course in that case she must verify God's differentia of a sainted companion; as we see in the Scripture, "whose beauty, let it not be the beauty of braided hair, wearing of gold, and putting on extra garments for show, i. e., no needless ornamentation; but let it be the hidden man of the heart, i. e., the creature created in the heart by the Holy Ghost in regeneration; in the purity of a meek and quiet spirit, which in the divine estimation is perfection complete; for in this way, the godly women in olden times were accustomed to adorn themselves, as Sarah, obeyed Abraham, calling him her lord, whose daughters you are, if true to the covenant." Here we see that the women who by nature excelled the men in beauty, are to abstain from all needless ornamentation, contenting themselves with the beauty of holiness. When I entered into wedlock with my dear companion fifty-five years ago, I thought her the most beautiful creature beneath the skies. What a wonderful change wrought by a half century and a half decade! those once raven locks turned to hoary grey, the rosy beauty of her angelic face, faded away; yet she appears to me more beautiful than ever; as the beauty of nature has simply retreated before that of holiness, which in every case infinitely eclipses it.

(k) Helen, the wife of Menelaus, the Grecian king, was celebrated as the most beautiful person in the nation. Paris, the son of Priam, the king of Troy, crossed the sea from the distant land of Asia and stole her away. He appealed to his comrade kings in the heroic land of Greece, to lend a helping hand in the redress of the intolerable insult from a foreign power; when they all heroically responded, and

with their armies sailed away and laid seige to old
Troy, which continued in bloody conflict, ten long
years, when the city was captured by the stratagem
of the wooden horse, invented by the crafty Ullyses,
the king of Ithaca and that ancient capital destroyed
and Greece impoverished of men and money, for
that one beautiful woman. As you see in Homer's
Iliad, those famous twenty-four poetical books, still
bearing the palm of the world, describing this me-
morable ten years' war:

"Achilles' wrath, to Greeks the direful spring,
Of woes unnumbered, heavenly goddesses sing;
That wrath that hulde to Pluto's gloomy reign,
The souls of mighty chiefs, untimely slain;
Whose bones unburied on the naked shore,
Devouring dogs' and hungry vultures' store.
Since great Atrides and Achilles strove,
 Such was the sovereign power,
And such the will of Jove,
Declare , oh Muse, in what ill-fated hour,
Sprang the fierce wrath, from what offended
  power;
Letona's so..n a dire contagion spread,
And heaped the camp with mountains of the
  dead."

(1) Adonis was pronounced the most beautiful
man in the world, so the Greeks deified him, and
as they stood at the front of the world in their day,
he received the adoration of all the earth with the
exception of the one nation, Israel, who had the
good fortune to know the Lord; thus delivered from
the awful woes, nominal to demoniacal worship, the
very essence of idolatry. Beauty in all ages and
nations has been cunningly manipulated by Satan,
to delude and ruin the countless millions. The ve-
nereal diseases, are the most afflictive and incurable

in the medical world, so named from Venus, the goddess of love and beauty, worshipped so copiously and recklessly throughout the heathen world in all ages.

Chapter Two.
AMBITION.

This the most irresistible and predominant of all temptation as we see abundantly illustrated in the fall of Lucifer, the great archangel, when he aspired to the divinity, seeking a division and participation of universal sovereignty, which belongs to God alone thus losing his hold on God and drifting indefinitely and eternally. Oh, how this temptation predominated in poor Absalom. See him riding out in his royal chariot, his person magnetizing all eyes with the royal flourish of his copious braided locks and every device calculated to charm the gazing rabble! fifty men running before him pursuant to the custom of the potent Oriental monarch, moving in panorama in his glowing imagination of his own royal pageantry, speedily pending. Thus playing king, he impressed all the people of his ambitious aspirations as coming events cast their shadows before; meanwhile he sent spies throughout the kingdom to peregrinate all lands and post up the people to be on the lookout for the rise of the new king in the succession of his father David, saying to them, "When you hear the trumpet blow every body shout, Absalom reigns in Hebron." Thus adroitly and clandestinely, he not only by flatteries, "steals the hearts of the people," but through these crafty subterranean manipulations, really has a universal expectancy of the contemplated change of administration. How strange, that David did not suspect, high treason thus through successive years, leavening the nation for the impending revolution! It can only be ac-

counted for by his profound fatherly affection for
his son, which never did evanesce, not even when
he came leading his great army against him at Ma-
hanaim as you see to the very last, he manifested
the most profound parental love, which seemed that
even years of high treason, could not dampen.

(m) When all arrangements were made through
the spies, dispersed throughout the kingdom, consummating the impending revolution; he goes to his
father and in loving, complacent, filial attitude, telling him that he had made a covenant with God while
in exile, that if He would deliver him and let him return unto his native land, he would serve Him faith-
fully forever, and he wanted to go to Hebron to offer a sacrifice, to the God of Abraham, Isaac, Jacob,
Joseph, Moses, Samuel and his own father David;
when he cheerfully acquiesces, saying, go in peace;
thus hypocritically covering his treacherous resolu-
tion with a grand religious festival, when really it
was a treacherous political barbecue. He manipu-
lates that a great host goes down from Jerusalem to
attend, the so-called holiness camp meeting, when it
was a treacherous conspiracy. There at Hebron,
with great pomp and pageantry, he is crowned king
in the succession of his father, 25 years antecedently crowned at that city the capital of Judah his own
tribe. The multitude is so great assembled hither
from all parts of the kingdom as to look like the
world is actually risen up and gone after Absalom;
not only charmed by his personal beauty, perfect
physical symmetry, without a solitary blemish, and
his brilliant impressive physiognomy, but the se-
ductive tide of popular adulation which he had been
turning on them for years, meeting them at the
gate, kissing and flattering them and impressing
them that he was the best friend they had in the

world, and if he were king he would grant them every conceivable favor.

(n) Of course the news flies on the wings of the wind, telegraphs and telephones undreamed of; so it reaches Jerusalem, that Absalom is coming with a vast army. David, himself the greatest military man in the world, knows that he is incompetent to protect the city from capture, and consequently vacating his throne, runs for his life accompanied by his body guards and a few faithful friends, having left the royal palace in charge of the ten matrons. He covers his head with sackcloth and weeps as he runs away barefoot, thus in the attitude of deepest grief, actually weeping aloud; accepting the calamity as a righteous judgment in the permissive providence of God, in just retribution for his maltreatment of Uriah, as he stood at the head of the holy nation; his evil example deserved the most summary castigation to alarm all others, in coming ages. His comrades, citizens and soldiers, sympathetically with him also weep and wail. Zadok and Abiathar, the priests come along bearing the ark of God, when he sends them back with it, as he was an old warrior thus adopting war strategy, which is not to be justified but may be cognomened a necessary evil, utilized by divine wisdom and mercy and overruled for good; as ye see the conspicuous part Judas and Pilate took in our Lord's crucifixion, utilized in His infallible providence, as Christ had come into the world to suffer and die, to redeem every son and daughter of Adam's ruined race and would have died if these men had never been born. So here we see these priests sent back to operate as spies in Absalom's camp, confirming their feigned sympathy with him, by returning to him the ark of God in their custodianship.

(o) He now meets Hushi, the Archite, greeting

him with fond enthusiasm and assuring him that he
can perfectly rely on him for anything in his power
to help him in his troubles, when he sends him
back to Jerusalem to co-operate with Zadok and Abiathar in their commission to conserve his interest in
Absalom's counsel; at the same time deputizing him
to defeat the counsel of Ahithophel, the Gilonite,
venerable and celebrated far and wide for his wisdom; all the people looking upon him as an inspired
oracle; receiving his **ipse dixit** as the edict of Jehovah.   Already Absalom in his capture of the lion's
part of Israel, had appropriated this wiseacre, who
had served him in his grand council at Hebron,
where they had crowned him king, in the succession of his father David; meanwhile he thus com-
missioned him to defeat the counsel of Ahithophel,
fervently sending up his prayer, "O Lord, turn the
counsel of Ahithophel into foolishness."

(p) Now Absalom, followed by his grand army
and a mighty host of congratulatory friends, enters
Jerusalem in imperial pomp and pageantry, proceed-
ing at once to the royal palace on Mt. Zion, where,
persuant to the counsel of Ahithophel, he officially
receives the ten matrons whom David had left in
charge of the palace; a tent having been spread on
the great flat roof, bannistered on all sides, the favorite recreation ground in the city, peculiar to
great Oriental houses and so conspicuous to the
vast multitude who thus see him formally take pos-
session of the palace, in the succession of his father,
thus confirming their anticipations of his royal coronation and glorious reign over all Israel.

(q) Now, of course, David and his men are to be
disposed of in some way, and Ahithophel proceeds at
once to solve the problem, suggesting to Absalom in
presence of all his senate, to send him with 12,000
men with all expedition to overtake his father in his

flight, before he has time to rendezvous an army, capture him, with all his concommitants, who will surrender at discretion; thus winding up the revolution and restoring universal peace and prosperity unto the reign of their favorite, Absalom. As Absalom understood that Hushi was with him, heart and hand, of course he compliments him with the opportunity to give counsel, if he has anything to say; when he proceeded to observe, "The counsel of Ahithophel is not good, because these men with your father are all valiant heroes, and will fight like a bear robbed of her whelps; they are his body guards, and old comrades in arms, while your men are raw recruits, and the result is, they will prove so heroic, that they will actually whip your 12,000, and, as to your father, no doubt, he is now hidden in a cave, and so you would n't get him, and the report would go out that Absalom's army is defeated, and David is still alive and all right, and his army victorious, and consequently every man's heart will melt within him and the cause will be lost, and Absalom's reign thus forever defeated." Then they say, "Well, what shall we do?"

(r) He proceeds to give counsel, "I suggest that we hold on till we can rendezvous all Israel from Dan to Beersheba, innumerable as the sands of the sea, and go against him under the leadership of Absalom in person and take him and all his comrades and thus settle the matter forever, or if he fortifies himself in a town, just put ropes around it and draw it, with everybody that dares to stay in it, into the river, and thus clear the field with unanimity for Absalom." Then they respond all around, Absalom with all the rest, "The counsel of Hushi is better than that of Ahithophel." The result was that Ahithophel was so broken-hearted that he mounted his donkey, went home to Giloh and hung himself; in his wonderful wisdom, doubtless, anticipating the awful disaster which really did follow, and the mournful fate and signal failure of the revolution, in which he had taken so active part, and consequently anticipating the collapse against him, destined to down him forever, gave up in despair and committed suicide.

(s) All this time Hushi, Zadok and Abiathar were just waiting the verdict of the counsel to give word to David, who was then on the plain of the wilderness opposite the Jordan ford, awaiting the tidings, which Ahimaaz and Jonathan, the sons of the priests, were waiting at Enrogel, outside of the city, to carry at post haste. They send the word to them by a "wench," i. e., a servant woman, whom none would suspect. However, a boy saw her and reported, and they sent after them; but they caught a suspicion and stopped at a house where the woman hid them in a well, laying plank over it and spreading a cloth, and putting on it ground barley for the sun to dry; so that when the pursuers reached it they looked all around, hunting them, and thinking this was simply an adjunct of the culinary department did not open it; but passed on, making inquiry as they went, and failing to hear a word, as night had fallen; concluding it was a mistake, came back; when she lets them out, and oh! how they run, fleeter than anybody in our day of steam and electricity; dashing with wonderful expedition till they reach David's camp, and nobody goes to bed, but all proceed and cross the Jordan that very night, pitching their tents at Mahanim.

Chapter Three.
HIS TRAGICAL DEATH

If they had followed the counsel of Ahithophel, the wiseacre of the age, it would have been signal disaster to David and triumphant success for Absalom, but God was in it all the way through, and that was the reason why they rejected it and followed the counsel of Hushi. God was not ready for David to give up the throne; though the elements all looked so dark that we do not wonder that the people rushed to the conclusion that the time had arrived when his brilliant and popular son was to succeed him. Shimei, the Benjamite, had execrated him so awfully, and thrown stones at him; meanwhile Abishai, the brother of Joab, was eager to slay him on the spot, but David would not let him, and told them to let him execrate him and thus abuse him, as it was a divine retribution to him for his maltreatment of Uriah, in order to terrify others and enforce the moral law in the palace as well as the hovel; Shimei, thinking that it was a judgment sent on him for maltreatment of King Saul, for which he was not guilty, as the Bible says he never disobeyed God except in the case of Uriah; therefore summary castigation was necessary to vindicate the divine administration from partiality, even in the highest circles of society; as Nathan had said to him, that the sword would never depart from his house; thus illustrating the inviolability of the divine law, a most valuable lesson to all the people who will ever live on the earth; a grand truth even so revealed by the light of nature that the heathen Roman poet, Horace, has left it for all to read: **Pena, claudo pede, nunquam deseruit criminis antecedentem,**—punishment, though with lame foot, is sure to overtake the criminal. This was all a divine retribution as well as so

many more troubles which came on him in his ad-
minstration.

(t) If they had followed the counsel of Ahithophel
those 12,000 men would have had no trouble to pick
up him and all he had and settle the matter in Absalom's favor.   While Absalom, persuant to the counsel of Hushi, postponed to rendezvous a great army;
the same time was, of course, utilized by David;
meanwhile his old friends who had known him all his
life, and the veterans who had fought in his army
rallied to him, till he really had all he needed; as the
battle took place in the Wood of Ephraim, so named
from the battle of Jephthai with the Ephraimites,
who live west of the river, but came thither to wage
war against him because he did not call them to his
war with the Ammonites, over whom he had achieved the great and signal victory; but suffered signal
defeat   and   was glad to skedaddle away,   when
42,000 of them perished at the Jordan Fords, when
they endeavored to cross and proved unable to pro-
nounce the password, "Shibboleth," but said, "Sibo-
leth."   As the record says that when Absalom arrived with his great army and fought in this tangled wood, that the brush slew more than the sword,
i. e., his great army proved unwieldy in the tangled
woods, whereas David's army, much smaller, and the
more expert, achieved a great victory, slaying 20,000
of Absalom's men; eventually Absalom in person
getting into close contact with David's mighty men,
who were cutting down everything before them, so
his mule takes fright and dashes under the thick
tangled branches of an elastic oak tree (in that country the oak, not brittle and straight as in America;
but exceedingly tenacious, twisty and crooked, the
limbs bent in acute angles in all directions, as on Mt.
Moriah when Abraham offered up Isaac, and God ar-
rested the stroke and had him spare him and showed

him a ram whose horns were fast in the bramble, so
he had nothing to do but take him and offer his sacrifice).

(u) Therefore that tangled forest was terrifically
detrimental to Absalom's great army, so largely raw
militia. The mule having dashed under this tangled
and matted oak tree, Absalom's head is caught fast
in those kinky, crooked limbs; his copious suit of
hair, so consummating the entanglement that he
could not get loose at all; the animal running off,
leaving him hanging by the neck; when a man tells
Joab and he says, "Why did you not shoot him at
once?" "Oh," says he, "I heard the king as we
passed out for the battle calling aloud and charging
us all not to hurt his son Absalom." Then Joab at
once runs and shoots three darts into his chest;
meanwhile his body guard proceed, kill him, and cast
him into a sink hole hard by, and they erect a great
heap of stones on him; when Joab blows a trumpet,
proclamatory of the battle over, when they all quit
fighting and rally around him, and he sends Cushi
to bear the news to David, who runs with all his
might, believed to be one of the ten, constituting
Joab's body guard, who killed Absalom; meanwhile
Ahimaaz, the young priest, who had with Jonathan
brought the word from Hushi, Zadok and Abiathar,
in Absalom's counsel, to David, to cross the river,
and prepare for war; begged Joab to let him bear
tidings, when he refused; but still he insisted so that
Joab consented, and he ran and passed Cushi on the
road, and arrived first of all when David was on the
tower looking for tidings. So Ahimaaz simply said,
"The battle is over and we are victorious," but could
not tell him anything about Absalom, as he did not
know.

(v) Soon Cushi comes with the awful news that
Absalom is dead, and David gives way to loud and

bitter wails, lugubrious cries and moans; all the people with him breaking down and crying too, as, wringing his hands and beating his breast, his mournful wail rang out, "Would to God I had died for thee, O Absalom, my son!" Look into an old copy of the "Missouri Harmony" and you will find David's lamentation over Absalom, words and notes as they sang it in my boyhood. While the victory of Mahanim was in every way glorious, there was no shouting over it, no bonfires, nor illuminations, nor any other ovations, manifesting the joy and rejoicing, normal to such occasions; as it seemed that David would die of grief for his son; all the people sympathetically, as they came to congratulate him over his victory and establishment in the kingdom, broke out weeping and wailing, a most abnormal way to celebrate a victory, never before heard of.

Chapter Four.

HIS MONUMENT.

He had two sons, but they passed away in childhood, leaving him with none to perpetuate his name, childless, except an only daughter, Tamar, whom he named for her disgraced aunt. Consequently in his life time he had a beautiful monument built, as the Bible says, "Pillar in the king's dale," still standing, and I have often seen it in the valley of Jehoshaphat at the western base of Mt. Olivet in full sight of the Garden of Gethsemane; a really nice elegantly hewn stone, conical edifice, somewhat in dilapidation, but it seems that there is nobody to repair it. Though the Jews are pouring into that country from all the ends of the earth by myriads in the delectable fulfillment of the latter day prophecies, and rebuilding all the old cities which were desolated during the Jewish tribulation, A. D. 66-73, so that they are leaping into life everywhere newly built beautiful stone edifices, from foundation to the slate roof; upper floors supported by stone arches and I have been astonished that they do not repair Absalom's monument, as it looks so lugubrious, reminding the traveler of his short and eventful life and tragical death. Though this is really a tombular monument, his remains were never put in it as they cast him into the sinkhole near the cruel oak tree that hung him and cast a great heap of rough irregular stones on him; oh, what a melancholy souvenir of his sad and mournful fate!

When young, life's journey I began,
The glittering prospects charmed my eyes;
I saw along the extended plain,
Joy after joy, successive rise;
But soon I found 'twas all a dream,
And learned the fond pursuit to shun;

> When few can reach their purposed aim,
> And thousands daily are undone!

(w) In Greek mythology, Apollo is the sun god, who drives his fiery chariot daily over the sky expelling the darkness; flooding the world with his glorious light; driving away the wintry cold, adorning the hills and valleys, mountains and plains with blooming flowers and wrapping them in the lovely green foliage; filling the world with luscious fruits, feeding man, beast and bird, from the grand, inexhaustible store houses of delicious fabulam; inundating land and sea with joy and gladness. The fable tells us, as we read in Ovid's poems, that Phaethon, his son concluded he would like to drive the fiery chariot over the sky, but the old man told him he was incompetent to manage the fiery steeds. But he kept begging, on and on, and teasing him till finally, worn out, patience gone, he flashed the flame over his face to inure him to the heat and light and let him mount and go ahead. At first he is wonderfully delighted with the ride up the azure vaults, looking down on oceans, seas and continents; perfectly electrified and so glad his father let him drive the chariot. Eventually the fiery steeds glancing back discover that the old man is not in his place, but it is the boy and consequently began to prance and lunge and charge; the boy castigating them with the whip which only made them worse, till they fled the track and got the sun down so near the earth till it was burning her up and actually made the great Sahara desert of Africa, in the Torrid zone, and other deserts, till Terra, the earth goddess, cried to Jupiter and walking out on the lofty firmament, he saw the trouble, that Apollo was not in his place and the boy was there, hurled a thunderbolt and knocked him whirling till he fell down on the earth in a dying condition, cripped for life, now the patient

of the sympathetic muses; and at once restored the
Solar chariot back to its place and Apollo to his seat
on the flaming vehicle, when every thing got right
as hitherto.

"Faith, and Phaeton once upon the ethereal plain
Leaped on his father's car and seized the reign;
Far from his track impelled the glowing sun,
Till Nature's laws to wild disorder run."

Chapter Five.
THE RESTORATION

As Judah, David's own tribe, who had first crowned him king seven and one-half years antecedently
to his coronation by all the other tribes at Jerusalem,
had led the way in the revolt; they now led the way
in his restoration; Joab, having waited long for David to quit mourning for Absalom and take his place
on the throne, readjust all the irregularities and proceed as in days of yore; finally found it necessary to
actually asume the dictatorship and just tell him
that if he did not quit mourning for Absalom and
take hold of the government and resume his place,
and thus give him a chance to restore everything,
that he would actually get into more trouble than
ever.   Then taking him at his word he acquiesced
and they proceed to readjust and restore everything;
David cheerfully and lovingly forgiving everybody
who had been led away by his unfortunate son in the
revolt against him; even Shimei who had so malig-
nantly execrated and thrown rocks at him and thus
clearing the way for everything appertaining to his
re-establishment in the kingdom; the ten matrons
with whom he had left the palace and who had so
signally disgraced themselves, philathopically retir-
ing from their offices and cared for as they might
need, and everything which had gotten out of kilter,
readjusted and restored.

(x) Though Judah had led the way in the revolt,
they now lead the way in the restitution; so promi-
nently as to arouse the suspicion of the other tribes,
lest they might take too much authority and the
government become an oligarchy instead of a kingdom in which all the tribes had equal rights and
privileges. Consequently there was a reaction, superinducing dissatisfaction on the part of the other
tribes, till he actually made war against Judah; in

which they were moving along in a terrible bloody
conflict; meanwhile Joab, the great and powerful
captain of David's army who had been so wonderfully used of the Lord in the conquest of all their
enemies, surrounding them on all sides and full of
prejudice against them because they were an isolat-
ed people and as they though claiming the pre-emi-
nence in all the world; refusing to intermarry with
their Gentile neighbors; thus looking on them as
dogs, and if they came in contact with them the law
of Moses made them ceremonially unclean until the
water of purification was sprinkled on the subject
of ceremonial defilement by some ceremonially clean
person; thus relegating all other nations actually on
par with the unclean animals; the camel, donkey,
horse, mule, dog, hog, etc. These distinctions reared
up a wall between the Jews and all the Gentile world,
actually insulting their majesty as they felt they
were just as good as the Jews; really Jerusalem with
her claim to be the holy city of the world was a constant rebuke to all of the nations, and consequently
they longed for her destruction and were all com-
bined against her. Under the leadership of Joab,
David had conquered them all. As Amasa had been
captain of the host under Absalom, during these
wars which seemed to normally supervene in the re-
instatement of David, Joab killed Amasa, and thus
again stood at the head of the Hebrew nation second
only to the king, as he was commander-in-chief.
Amid the perturbations, Sheba became a prominent
leader and when everything had tranquilized down,
so there was no reason why peace should not univer-
sally reign, he with his followers still remained bel-
ligerent evidently actuated by insurrectionary mo-
tives, finally taking refuge with his follwers in a
city, which Joab with his army proceeds to besiege
and is pressing things hard when a wise woman

shouts aloud to him and he hears her, over the wall, "Oh, Joab, will you not spare a mother in Israel and thousands of innocent people in this city!" When he shouts back, "Oh yes, I only want Sheba." When she shouts back, "Be patient and we will throw you his head over the wall." She presents the matter to the princesses of the city and soon the gory head is thrown over the wall and Joab blows his trumpet, signifying the victory won, the war over and universal peace, David reinstated and all right.

THE END.